Frida Kahlo
❧ Folding Screen ❧

Milánkovi věnuje babička
Mourilová

1993.

Chronicle Books • San Francisco

⚜

Printed in Singapore
Produced and designed by Marquand Books, Inc.
ISBN: 0-8118-0176-4

Works by Frida Kahlo are reproduced with permission of the
Instituto Nacional de Bellas Artes, Mexico City

Distributed in Canada by
Raincoast Books
112 East 3rd Avenue
Vancouver, B.C. V5T1C8

1 3 5 7 9 10 8 6 4 2

Chronicle Books
275 Fifth Street
San Francisco, California 94103

*Self-Portrait with Portrait of
Dr. Juan Farill,* 1951
Private collection (Mexico)

The Two Fridas, 1939
Museo de Arte Moderno, Mexico City

Self-Portrait, 1948
Private collection (Mexico)

The Love Embrace of the Universe . . . , 1949
Jacques and Natasha Gelman Collection

PARA MARTE R. GOMEZ, CARIÑOSAMENTE. DIBUJÓ FRIDA KAHLO. DIC. 1946. MÉXICO

FRIDA KAHLO

Self-Portrait with Monkeys, 1943
Jacques and Natasha Gelman Collection

Self-Portrait with Necklace, 1933
Jacques and Natasha Gelman Collection

Thinking of Death, 1943
Private collection (Mexico)

Self-Portrait as a Tehuana
(Diego in My Thoughts), 1943
Jacques and Natasha Gelman Collection

***Self-Portrait Dedicated
to Sigmund Firestone*, 1940**
Collection of Violet Gershenson, New York

***Self-Portrait Wearing a Velvet Dress*, 1926**
**Collection of Alejandro Gómez Arias,
Mexico City**

***Self-Portrait with Braid*, 1941**
Jacques and Natasha Gelman Collection

***Self-Portrait Dedicated to Marte R. Gómez*, 1946**
**Collection of Marte Gómez Leal,
Mexico City**

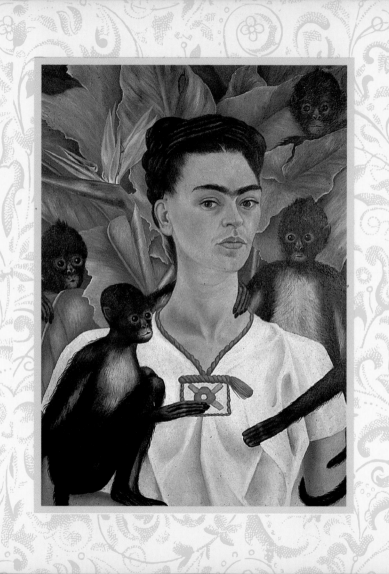